the art of
marriage®
C O N N E C T

enjoying your marriage in the second half

Mike and Linda Montgomery

FamilyLife Publishing®
Little Rock, Arkansas

Enjoying Your Marriage in the Second Half
FamilyLife Publishing®
5800 Ranch Drive, Little Rock, Arkansas 72223
1-800-FL-TODAY • FamilyLife.com
FLTI, d/b/a FamilyLife®, is a ministry of Campus Crusade for Christ International®

ISBN: 978-1-60200-685-0

Design: Faceout® Studio
Images: iStockphoto, Shutterstock, Thinkstock, and Faceout Studio

Printed in the United States of America

22 21 20 19 18   1 2 3 4 5

FAMILYLIFE®

*Unless the Lord builds the house,
those who build it labor in vain.*

—PSALM 127:1

The Art of Marriage® Connect Series

Building Your Marriage to Last
Improving Communication in Your Marriage
Building Teamwork in Your Marriage
Enjoying Your Marriage in the Second Half
Resolving Conflict in Your Marriage
Growing Together in Christ
Building up Your Spouse

welcome to the
art of marriage connect

Marriage should be enjoyed, not endured. It is meant to be a vibrant relationship between two people who love each other with passion, commitment, understanding, and grace. So secure is the bond God desires between a husband and a wife that He uses it to illustrate the magnitude of Christ's love for the church (Ephesians 5:25–33).

Do you have that kind of love in your marriage?

Relationships often fade over time as people drift apart—but only if the relationship is left unattended. We have a choice in the matter; our marriages don't have to grow dull. Perhaps we just need to give them some attention.

That's the purpose behind the Art of Marriage® Connect (AOMC) Series—to provide you a way to give your marriage the attention it needs and deserves. This small-group study is biblically based because, in the Bible, God has given the design for building a loving and secure marriage. His plan enables a man and a woman to grow together in a mutually satisfying relationship and then to reach out to others with the love of Christ. Ignoring God's plan may lead to isolation and, in far too many cases, the breakup of the home.

Whether your marriage needs a complete makeover or just a few small adjustments, we encourage you to consult God's design. Although written nearly two thousand years ago, the Bible still speaks clearly and powerfully about the conflicts and challenges men and women face.

Do we really need to be part of a group? Couldn't we just go through this study as a couple?

While you could work through the study as a couple, you would miss the opportunity to connect with friends and to learn from one another's experiences. You will find that the questions in each session not only help you grow closer to your spouse, but they also create an environment of warmth and fellowship with other couples as you study together.

What does it take to lead an AOMC group?

Leading a group is much easier than you may think, because the leader is simply a facilitator who guides the participants through the discussion questions. You are not teaching the material but are helping the couples discover and apply biblical truths. The special dynamic of an AOMC group is that couples teach themselves.

The study guide you're holding has all the information and guidance you need to participate in or lead an AOMC group. You'll find leader's notes in the back of the guide.

What is the typical schedule?

Most studies in the Art of Marriage Connect Series are six to eight weeks long, indicated by the number of sessions in the guide. The sessions are designed to take sixty minutes in the group with a project for the couples to complete between sessions.

Isn't it risky to talk about your marriage in a group?

The group setting should be enjoyable and informative—and nonthreatening. THREE SIMPLE GROUND RULES will help ensure that everyone feels comfortable and gets the most out of the experience:

1. Don't share anything that will embarrass your spouse.
2. You may pass on any question you do not want to answer.
3. If possible, complete the couple's project between group sessions.

What other help does FamilyLife® offer?

Our list of marriage and family resources continues to grow. Visit FamilyLife.com to learn more about our

- Weekend to Remember® marriage getaway, The Art of Marriage®, Stepping Up®,FamilyLife Blended™, and other live conferences and hosted events;
- slate of radio broadcasts, including the nationally syndicated *FamilyLife Today®*, *Real FamilyLife® with Dennis Rainey*, and *FamilyLife This Week®*;
- multimedia resources for small groups, churches, and community networking;
- interactive products for parents, couples, blended families, small-group leaders, and one-to-one mentors; and
- blogs, forums, and other online connections.

about the authors

Mike and Linda Montgomery were high school sweethearts and have been married since 1970. Twenty-three years were spent moving around the world as an Air Force family until Mike's retirement as a colonel in 1995. They are the parents of two married children and, if asked, are sure to tell you about their grandchildren. Mike and Linda are directors for Cru Military in the Virginia Peninsula, where they live and serve all five branches of the military. Their mission is to train military couples to build strong marriages and leave the lasting legacy of Christian homes.

about the general editors

Dennis and Barbara Rainey are cofounders of FamilyLife. Authors of over twenty-five book and hundreds of articles, they are also popular conference speakers and radio hosts. With six grown children and numerous grandchildren, the Raineys love to encourage couples in building godly marriages and families.

contents

on enjoying your marriage in the second half

Whenever someone describes their marriage by saying, "It just keeps getting better," I know one of two things is true: they are still on their honeymoon, or they give their marriage the attention it needs no matter how many anniversaries they've celebrated.

Okay, that's an oversimplification, but you get my point. If you want your marriage to get better through the years, you have to keep working at it. Slackers make terrible spouses.

Every marriage has its own set of challenges, but the onset of the empty nest and retirement—the second half of marriage—is an almost universal season of struggle for couples. Without awareness and good use of God's designs, spouses may find themselves drifting apart and joyless just as they are entering a time of great opportunity. But it doesn't have to be that way. It really can keep getting better.

Mike and Linda Montgomery are in their second half, and I have to say that I admire the way they love and serve. I believe you can greatly benefit from the insights and counsel they offer in this study. These are not untried theories, but reliable teachings taken directly from Scripture—God's master designs for marriage.

—Dennis and Barbara Rainey,
General Editors

~1~

Threats to Oneness

You can face the second-half years of your marriage in joyful anticipation of what the Lord can do to strengthen oneness between you and your spouse and to pass along a legacy of faith. You can finish well!

warm-up

Introduce yourself to the group. Briefly tell how you met your spouse and what attracted you to him or her.

Share a favorite memory from your early years of marriage.

master designs

Before looking ahead, take the opportunity to look back. Most couples have experienced challenges that were not expected when they pledged their marriage vows. Many wish they had been better prepared for those challenges.

1. Share one lesson you have learned as a couple that you can apply to the potential challenges ahead.

Wisdom is found in taking lessons from our past and applying them to what we face in the present and future. Wisdom is also found in recognizing dangers to your unity as a married couple. For example, ask yourselves: What changes are difficult for us to face and accept? What priorities have we disagreed on in the past and which ones continue to provoke conflict? What attitudes have been harmful to our relationship through the years? Differences in these three areas can restrict your ability to move forward together and can threaten your oneness in the second half.

Threat #1: Difficult Transitions

Transitions are unavoidable in midlife marriages. Some couples will shift from full-time work to retirement years, perhaps from an active lifestyle to one limited by health concerns. Others might encounter demands from adult children, grandchildren, or elder caregiving.

2. What transitions have you noticed within your circle of friends?

3. We may have wonderful expectations for what our later years will look like. While those expectations may become reality, oftentimes they are dampened by unanticipated circumstances or events. How have your attitudes about transitions been affected by your expectations?

Threat #2: Differing Priorities

Being on the same page as a couple means being in agreement so that what is important to one spouse is important to the other. Oneness grows from identifying those mutual priorities and determining what will occupy your time, your financial investments, and your future plans.

Case Study

Just when Ray reached retirement, the grandchildren started arriving. His wife, Lydia, wanted time with the little ones, but Ray wanted time with her for travel and recreation.

4. What adjustments can Ray and his wife make in order to maintain a proper focus on their marriage?

Threat #3: Divisive Attitudes

A marriage is strengthened when a husband and wife commit to persevere through difficult transitions, make unity a priority, and battle divisiveness brought on by unhelpful or hurtful attitudes. You can be steadfast in your commitment by continuing to focus together on God's purposes for marriage in Genesis 2:24, "Therefore a man shall leave his father and his mother and hold fast to his wife, and they shall become one flesh."
Scripture clearly identifies attitudes that build oneness.

Put on then, as God's chosen ones, holy and beloved, compassion, kindness, humility, meekness, and patience, bearing with one another and, if one has a complaint against another, forgiving each other; as the Lord has forgiven you, so you also must forgive. And above all these put on love, which binds everything together in perfect harmony. And let the peace of Christ rule in your hearts, to which indeed you were called in one body. And be thankful. (Colossians 3:12–15)

5. From the Colossians 3 passage, identify nine positive attitudes that build oneness in marriage.

6. Who is the standard for these attitudes?

> If you have any encouragement from being united with Christ, if any comfort from his love, if any fellowship with the Spirit, if any tenderness and compassion, then make my joy complete by being like-minded, having the same love, being one in spirit and purpose. Do nothing out of selfish ambition or vain conceit, but in humility consider others better than yourselves. Each of you should look not only to your own interests, but also to the interests of others. (Philippians 2:1–4 NIV)

7. According to Philippians 2, how does an unselfish attitude manifest itself in marriage?

8. What else does oneness in Christian marriage mean besides a physical union?

keystone principle

Commitment in marriage includes
developing unity of action and attitude.

Close your group time together with this benediction from Jude 24–25:

Now to him who is able to keep you from stumbling and to present you blameless before the presence of his glory with great joy, to the only God, our Savior, through Jesus Christ our Lord, be glory, majesty, dominion, and authority, before all time and now and forever. Amen.

make a date

Set a time for you and your spouse to complete the couple's project together before the next group meeting.

....
date

....
time

....
location

Scan this code for additional content.

Or visit FamilyLife.com/connect.

couple's project

On Your Own

1. During the group session, you discussed three threats to a mid-life marriage: difficult transitions, differing priorities, and divisive attitudes. Reflect on how these three threats have affected your marriage. Circle the appropriate number (1 being the least threatening and 5 the most) to note the impact of this threat on your marriage in the past. Then briefly describe how this threat could impact your marriage in the future.

Threats	Severity	Future Impact
Difficult transitions	1 2 ③-④ 5	3+4
Differing priorities	1 2 ③ ④ 5	3+4
Divisive attitudes	1 ②③ 4 5	2+3

2. What difficult transitions are you experiencing right now or believe you will be facing soon?

   - January when I change depts at work again

3. List one thing you will do this week to demonstrate the priority of your marriage.

   - put food in the crockpots
   = making sure your white clothes are clean
   = put stuff on Craigs list

4. List some of your spouse's positive attitudes that have affected your marriage.

   - supports whatever decision I make about my jobs
   - emotionaly supported me through school
   - listen to me when I'm feeling un atractive

With Your Spouse

1. Share your answers from the questions you answered on your own. How can you help each other recognize the threats to oneness in your marriage?

2. Describe a time in your marriage when you felt especially close to each other.

— When Bruce defends me when I feel people are not being nice to me.

3. What factors contributed to that feeling of closeness?

Because I have never felt like anyone has consistantly defended me

4. Pray with each other to grow in oneness during this study as God reveals His will for your life together.

Remember to take your calendar to the next session for Make a Date.

Recommended Resources

The Art of Marriage® from FamilyLife

Lost in the Middle: Midlife and the Grace of God by Paul David Tripp

Fight Fair: Winning at Conflict Without Losing at Love by Tim and Joy Downs

Staying Close: Stopping the Natural Drift Toward Isolation in Marriage by Dennis and Barbara Rainey

Weekend to Remember® marriage getaway from FamilyLife

~2~
Live Well

The life lessons you learn help set your priorities, plans, and purposes, while also strengthening your marriage.

warm-up

Choose one of the following to share with your group:

- Describe one helpful life lesson you learned from a grandparent or an elderly person. *Everything will come out in the wash. Choices*
- Describe one life lesson you would like to pass down to future generations. *His mercies are new every morning. Life is Choices*

Project Report

Share one thing you learned from the couple's project from last session.

master designs

Scripture says, "For the LORD gives wisdom; from his mouth come knowledge and understanding" (Proverbs 2:6). Learning truth from Scripture helps us to grow in wisdom throughout our lifetime.

Learning About Life from God's Word

1. Read aloud the following verses. Match each *do* and *don't* to its corresponding passage.

____ 1 Peter 4:8   A. Don't presume on wealth

____ 1 Thessalonians 5:16–18   B. Do avoid immorality

____ Hebrews 13:4   C. Do love

____ Luke 12:15   D. Don't presume on time

____ James 4:13–15   E. Don't worry

____ Matthew 6:25–27   F. Do be joyful, prayerful, and thankful

2. Read 2 Timothy 3:16–17, "All Scripture is breathed out by God and profitable for teaching, for reproof, for correction, and for training in righteousness, that the man of God may be competent, equipped for every good work."

Describe the various ways Scripture can shape our lives.

Learning the Lesson of Contentment

Contentment is one area many struggle with in midlife. Perhaps life didn't turn out like you thought, or you wish you had done better at such and such. Some discontentment is due to unrealistic expectations and some because of a struggle with acceptance.

A 14-year-old boy wrote the following poem, entitled "Present Tense," in 1989.

Read this piece aloud, and then answer the questions that follow.

Present Tense

It was spring, but it was summer I wanted,
The warm days, and the great outdoors.
It was summer, but it was fall I wanted,
The colorful leaves, and the cool, dry air.
It was fall, but it was winter I wanted,
The beautiful snow, and the joy of the holiday season.
It was winter, but it was spring I wanted,
The warmth and the blossoming of nature.
I was a child, but it was adulthood I wanted,
The freedom and respect.
I was 20, but it was 30 I wanted,
To be mature, and sophisticated.
I was middle-aged, but it was 20 I wanted,
The youth and the free spirit.
I was retired, but it was middle-age I wanted,
The presence of mind without limitations.
My life was over, and I never got what I wanted.[1]

3. Can you relate to this boy's attitude? How so?

4. In what ways do you see evidence of discontentment in our culture?

— feeling like they don't have enough money.

— divorce

—

The circumstances of the apostle Paul's life were anything but easy (2 Corinthians 11:24–28); he explains the secret of his contentment in Philippians 4:11–13:

Not that I am speaking of being in need, for I have learned in whatever situation I am to be content. I know how to be brought low, and I know how to abound. In any and every circumstance, I have learned the secret of facing plenty and hunger, abundance and need. I can do all things through him [Christ] who strengthens me.

5. According to these verses, how can a person be content no matter the circumstances?

— focus on Christ

— Choose to focus on Christ

— Choose to be dependent of Christ

— choose to trust + believe that I can do all things through Christ

Being content is a spiritual exercise developed through knowing God and His Word. Ultimately, we experience contentment by changing our attitude—from one of complaining to one of gratitude—more than from a change in our circumstances. Understanding God's sovereign control over our life brings us to a humble acceptance of His plan—which sometimes differs from our plan; His plan is always better.

Learning for a Lifetime

Learning for a lifetime means being willing to grow mentally and spiritually even as we are slowing down physically. It means being "teachable," which is a sign of maturity. As Steve Farrar writes in *Finishing Strong*, "If you're not teachable, you don't have a chance in the world of finishing strong. Not a chance."[2]

6.   What lessons about learning for a lifetime do we find in the following verses?

"Only take care, and keep your soul diligently, lest you forget the things that your eyes have seen, and lest they depart from your heart all the days of your life. Make them known to your children and your children's children." (Deuteronomy 4:9)

Give instruction to a wise man, and he will be still wiser; teach a righteous man, and he will increase in learning. (Proverbs 9:9)

7.   List some practical ways to remain teachable.

— Be willing to listen
— To be willing to look at another point with an open mind
— don't say out loud my truth is the only truth

Having a teachable spirit leads you to a desire to learn from Scripture. Intentionally spending time daily with the Lord in Bible reading and prayer will help you grow in knowledge of Him. Learning what God has to say in the Bible prepares you for difficulties in life. You should be willing to listen to what God wants to teach you and be committed to pray together for answers.

Dennis Rainey said, "If there is one simple ritual I would urge couples to begin adopting in their marriages, it is this one—the habit of praying together every day." Prayer is something you can learn. A disciple once approached Jesus with this request: "Lord, teach us to pray" (Luke 11:1). As God speaks to you through the Holy Spirit and the Bible, so you can speak with Him through prayer.

The acronym ACTS represents a way to model our prayer time with the Lord:

Adoration—praise and worship God

Confession—confess our personal sins to God

Thanksgiving—offer thanks to God

Supplication—petition God with our requests

8. Take time with your group to share ideas on how to make Bible study and prayer part of your daily life together as a couple

— *after Bruce gets out of shower around 6:30 pm*

The best place to learn to practice spiritual disciplines, including prayer, is in a godly home or at a Bible-believing church.

Of all the leadership decisions I have made by the grace of God, the very best one has been leading my wife and family into our local church . . . We are a part of it. It is a part of us and our entire family. For us, life, marriage, and raising children apart from the local church is literally unimaginable. Friends, this should be the norm, not the exception, for every Christian. And regardless of the cultural whirlwind around us, it is the local church—Christians living a shared life biblically before God and one another—that will ultimately secure the place and role of marriage and family from generation to generation.[3]

9. How important is the church in your family's life? What do you enjoy about worshipping together in your church?

— I enjoy the words of Knowledge
— people are free to quote a scripture
that the Lord lays on their heart

keystone principle

Living well includes learning well, for a lifetime.

Close your group time together with this benediction: "Now to him who is able to do far more abundantly than all that we ask or think, according to the power at work within us, to him be glory in the church and in Christ Jesus throughout all generations, forever and ever. Amen" (Ephesians 3:20–21).

make a date

Set a time for you and your spouse to complete the couple's project together before the next group meeting.

....
date

....
time

....
location

Scan this code for additional content.

Or visit FamilyLife.com/connect.

couple's project

On Your Own

1. The Lord gave his life so I could be saved

1. Spend time assessing the level of contentment in your life. List five things for which you are grateful to God.

2. The Lord gave a christian Man

3. The Lord gave me a beautiful home + Bruce to serve

4. The Lord has supplied me with a good job

5. The Lord has my children in my life so I can be Jesus with shin on

2. How would you rank your current level of spiritual growth? (Check the answer that best describes you.)

___ I don't give it any thought or concern.

___ I think about it occasionally, but rarely do anything about it.

___ I'm inconsistent, but more regress than progress.

___ I'm inconsistent, but more progress than regress.

___ I am seeking to grow spiritually stronger every day.

✓ Im consistent

3. Reflect on your group time. What ideas for Bible study and prayer would you like to implement in your marriage?

– 6:30 devotional pause/worship/prayer

Read this case study to understand how a simple prayer can help you to mature spiritually.

─────────────── **Case Study** ───────────────

Lydia knew that her mother needed help—she was getting weaker and unable to accomplish normal tasks. The family decided that Ray and Lydia would be her primary caregivers, a role they gladly accepted. But Lydia's relationship with her mom had never been close—nor was her relationship with her siblings a good one. As time went on, Lydia became resentful of the responsibilities she and Ray were given, without any support from family members. The day came when Lydia recognized her bitterness. She prayed a short, honest prayer: "Lord, I am bitter. Please forgive me." This simple prayer opened up her heart to receive God's forgiveness and to seek forgiveness with others, including her mother. She felt free from resentment and bitterness. She began to live in grace and thankfulness for the ways God had blessed her and carried her throughout her life. Nothing changed, but everything changed.

Confession is powerful—and can open the door to change in your heart. You can move from bitterness, to owning responsibility, to asking God for forgiveness, to accepting His gifts of grace.

4. Spend time in ACTS prayer (see p. 16 for a description).

With Your Spouse

1. Begin your time together in prayer. If you prefer, use the ACTS prayer model.

2. Discuss each of the following topics. Agree on a decision or action point for each one:

- Vacation—Is there a place we have always wanted to visit?
- Recreation—Are there some recreational activities that you enjoy and would like us to spend more time doing together?
- Romance—Are we spending time courting each other? Are we satisfied with our romantic life together?
- Intimacy—Are we satisfied with our level of intimacy? (Health, attitudes, aging, and some medications can affect the quality of intimacy, especially in midlife.)
- Legal Documents—Are our wills and other legal matters up to date?
- Insurance—Are we properly covered for health care and emergencies?
- Banking and Investments—Have we shared account information and passwords with each other?
- Church and/or Mission Involvement—Are we plugged in at our local church? Do we feel called to be involved in a new way at church or on a mission trip?
- Everyday Tasks—Are we satisfied with the division of chores at home?
- Household Projects—Is there work you or I would like to accomplish around the house?
- Extended Family—Are we satisfied with the level of involvement with extended family?
- Education—Is there a course you or I would like to take in order to learn a new skill or gain knowledge?
- Technology—What tools of modern technology are intimidating to us?
- Fears—What are we afraid of as we approach this season of life?

Close your time together in prayer, or proceed to the next project.

Having "The Talk" (optional)

At some point in time, all couples need to prepare for end-of-life issues. No one wants to have this conversation, but it will make things much easier for the surviving spouse if plans and desires are known in advance. We encourage couples to have "The Talk" before there is an apparent need, if possible. Issues to discuss include

- If it ever becomes an issue, what are your desires regarding being placed on life support?
- Where do you want to be buried? (Include other related arrangements.)
- Do you have any specific desires for a memorial service (pallbearers, music, scripture, speakers, etc.)?
- Do you have anything you want to communicate to me about my life as a widow/widower?

Remember to take your calendar to the next session for Make a Date.

Recommended Resources

Before the Last Resort by Dr. George Kenworthy
Mastering Money in Your Marriage, Resolving Conflict in Your Marriage from FamilyLife
The Art of Marriage® by FamilyLife
Moments With You by Dennis and Barbara Rainey
FamilyLife.com

~3~
Remember Well

Remembering your past can bring rejoicing, regret, or both. How a couple deals with the past affects their marriage in the second half.

warm-up

Share with your group a favorite memory from a childhood Christmas.

Also, share with your group a Christmas tradition you began as a couple.

Project Report

Share one thing you learned from the couple's project from last session.

master designs

Midlife can be a special time to examine God's ways in your lives. When you reflect on who He is and His faithfulness to you, your faith in God grows. As your faith grows, you become stronger spiritually and build endurance. This leads toward developing a more Christlike character and building hope for the future.

Remembering God's Faithfulness

The Bible is filled with stories of God's faithfulness to His people—from creation to His provision for salvation.

In one story of His faithfulness, God led the Israelites through the desert for forty years. Read Nehemiah 9:19–21.

> Because of your great compassion you did not abandon
> them in the desert. By day the pillar of cloud did not cease

to guide them on their path, nor the pillar of fire by night to shine on the way they were to take. You gave your good Spirit to instruct them. You did not withhold your manna from their mouths, and you gave them water for their thirst. For forty years you sustained them in the desert; they lacked nothing, their clothes did not wear out nor did their feet become swollen (NIV).

1. In what ways was God faithful to provide for His people of Israel?

— *God supplied all their physical needs even when they didn't believe or feared He wouldn't*

2. Share an example of God's faithfulness in your marriage.

— *when we make a questionable decision He comes through*

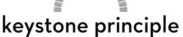

keystone principle

Remembering God's faithfulness in your life builds your faith and encourages you to face future challenges.

Case Study

Read the case study aloud and answer the questions that follow.

Ray had the opportunity to remember God's faithfulness when he attended his father's funeral. His dad had lived a troubled life, but came to faith in Jesus Christ when Ray was a teenager. The difference that life change made in their household was dramatic, and Ray never forgot.

Because of his dad's loving-kindness toward his mother, their marriage became a model for Ray and his wife, Lydia.

Because of what he remembered of his dad's conversion, it seemed appropriate to Ray that the hymn "Amazing Grace" was sung at the funeral. He listened carefully to the words, as if hearing them for the first time. "Amazing grace, how sweet the sound, that saved a wretch like me. I once was lost but now am found—was blind but now I see."

The pastor explained that those words were penned by John Newton—a captain of slave ships in the mid-1700s. Fearful of death during one particularly fierce storm at sea, Newton ultimately became aware of his sinfulness, repented, and surrendered his life to Jesus Christ. That story impacted Ray, who was wrestling with many feelings—even wondering if it was possible for the Lord to forgive him of mistakes he had made in his own life.

First John 1:8–9 says, "If we say we have no sin, we deceive ourselves, and the truth is not in us. If we confess our sins, [God] is faithful and just to forgive us our sins and to cleanse us from all unrighteousness."

3. Identify the truths in the 1 John passage that would encourage Ray.

God forgives all sin

4. Read Ephesians 4:32, "Be kind to one another, tenderhearted, forgiving one another, as God in Christ forgave you."

How does this verse describe the peace that came into Ray's parents' home years ago?

Remembering God's Faithfulness Builds Hope for the Future

Read 2 Corinthians 5:17, "Therefore, if anyone is in Christ, he is a new creation. The old has passed away; behold, the new has come."

> "A happy marriage is the union of two good forgivers."
> —Ruth Bell Graham

5. In what ways does this verse describe the change in John Newton and in Ray's dad?

Taking the time to reflect on the past and repent of sin can transform your life.

Case Study

Ray picked up a little booklet in the church after the funeral. When he had time to sit down and reflect, he chose to read this booklet—about how to know God personally.

Read the case study aloud.

He had come to grips with his own sinfulness and realized his sin caused him to feel distant from God. But what Ray read said that it was Jesus Christ who could bridge that distance. Through His death on the cross, Jesus had paid the penalty. His gift of salvation and reconciliation with God was available and free. The truth from Romans 5:8 made sense to Ray: "But God demonstrates His own love for us in this: While we were still sinners, Christ died for us" (NIV).

Ray began to understand why there had been peace in his home after his dad became a Christian. He bowed his head and read the short prayer written in the booklet: *Lord Jesus, I want to know You personally. Thank You for dying on the cross for my sins. I open the door of my life and receive You as my Savior and*

Lord. Thank You for forgiving me of my sins and giving me eternal life. Take control of the throne of my life. Make me the kind of person You want me to be.

Ray went on to read that he was now empowered by the Holy Spirit, Jesus Himself living inside his heart. He would now have the power to deal with the challenges ahead, because he was a child of God . . . in whom he had faith and could trust with his very life.

keystone principle

*However you remember your past, it is imperative
that you have a personal relationship with
Jesus Christ in order to truly live well.*

6. John 3:16 can be personalized to reflect Ray's decision to accept Jesus Christ. "For God so loved [Ray] that he gave his only Son, that [Ray] should not perish but have eternal life."

> "The most important decision you will ever make is to give your life to Christ and become His follower."
> —Billy Graham

Take time to pray in silence, using John 3:16. Pray for yourself or for someone who has not yet made that decision for salvation and transformation.

The remaining verses of the hymn "Amazing Grace" affirm the conversion which Ray experienced:

T'was grace that taught my heart to fear,
and grace my fears relieved;
How precious did that grace appear
the hour I first believed.

Through many dangers, toils and snares,
I have already come;
'Tis grace hath brought me safe thus far,
And grace will lead me home.

When we've been there ten thousand years,
Bright shining as the sun,
We've no less days to sing God's praise
Than when we first begun.

If you desire to know more about God's solution to our sin problem—and how to know God personally—turn to page 57.

Close your group time together with this benediction, "The Lord bless you and keep you; the Lord make his face to shine upon you and be gracious to you; the Lord lift up his countenance upon you and give you peace" (Numbers 6:24–26).

make a date

Set a time for you and your spouse to complete the couple's project together before the next group meeting.

....
date

....
time

....
location

Scan this code for additional content.

Or visit FamilyLife.com/connect.

couple's project

On Your Own

Answer the following questions:

1. What did you learn in the group session this week?

2. In what ways can you see God's faithfulness in your life? Does knowing that He has been faithful in the past help you to trust Him with your future?

   — we have an abundance — all of our needs are/have been taken care of and we have some left over.

   — unfortunately no — I say all the right things but I worry about things

3. Respond to the following statements with either *Y* (yes) or *N* (no):

   Y I have thanked God for His faithfulness in my life.

   Y I am secure in my relationship with Jesus Christ.

   Y I know where I am going to spend eternity.

4. Read Romans 10:9–10: If you confess with your mouth that Jesus is Lord and believe in your heart that God raised him from the dead, you will be saved. For with the heart one believes and is justified, and with the mouth one confesses and is saved.

If you gave your life to Jesus Christ during your group time, please write down the date. Be sure to tell someone—perhaps the leader of your group—or someone else you respect who can assist you in taking steps of growing in your faith.

5. Many Christians have found it meaningful to spend time alone with God, asking Him to reveal any sin that has not been confessed before Him. The following steps are recommended:[1]

- Get a sheet of paper and title it "For God's Eyes Only." Prayerfully list any actions and attitudes in your life that are contrary to God's Word and purposes. Focus on areas that affect your spouse.
- After a time of self-examination, write the words of 1 John 1:9 across your list, thanking God for His absolute forgiveness of all that you have done in the past and will do in the future.
- Thank Him for sending His Son to the cross to die for your sin.
- It may be necessary and appropriate for you also to confess to your spouse any attitudes or actions that have been harmful to him or her. Caution: If you are unsure about the appropriateness of sharing something, seek wise counsel before doing so.
- Destroy the page.
- Bow in prayer, and acknowledge God's authority over your life.

Let this quote from Dietrich Bonhoeffer encourage you during this project:

In a word, live together in the forgiveness of your sins, for without it no human fellowship, least of all a marriage, can survive. Don't insist on your rights, don't blame each other, don't judge or condemn each other, don't find fault with each other, but accept each other as you are, and forgive each other every day from the bottom of your hearts. From the first day of your wedding till the last the rule must be: "Welcome one another . . . for the glory of God." That is God's word for your marriage. Thank God for it; thank God for leading you thus far; ask God to establish your marriage, to confirm it, sanctify it, and preserve it. So your marriage will be "for the praise of God's glory." Amen.[2]

With Your Spouse

1. Discuss how you have seen God's faithfulness in your marriage. How does that knowledge help you trust Him with your marriage in the future? *Because we want to please him*
   - Kept / keeps us from calling each other demeaning names while during knock down drag out fights
   - I trust Him because Bruce is sold out to Christ + is led by the holy Spirit.

2. Share any struggles with your purpose in life that you are now experiencing at midlife.
   - The way I look
   - noting that I am the oldest in my department
   - other arthritis

3. Pray with each other for God to bring peace to your marriage and bless your future together.

Remember to take your calendar to the next session for Make a Date.

Recommended Resources

The Five Love Languages of Apology by Dr. Gary Chapman
    and Jennifer Thomas
Nearing Home by Billy Graham
The Second Half of Marriage by David and Claudia Arp
Torn Asunder by Dave Carder

~4~
Love Well

warm-up

Read this quote aloud:

> We teach couples to hold hands when walking, shopping,
> and sitting in church, even attending funerals! Remember
> God has called you and your mate to be as one. Show it. .
> . When you hold hands, you are telling the world You are
> in love; God was right in bringing you two together; You
> are fulfilling God's plan by filling each other's gaps (hands
> clasped together). You need each other's strengths and
> weaknesses; You want to honor God by your commitment to
> each other.[1]

What feelings do you get when you see an elderly couple holding
hands?

Tell about a favorite song that was "yours" during your time of
dating. *Moonlight Serenade*

Project Report

Share one thing you learned from last session's couple's project.

master designs

Love Sings

Using a musical metaphor, you could say that marriage starts out with a husband and wife agreeing to "sing from the same song sheet" until death separates them. But chords of turmoil and distrust can enter into the harmony of the relationship. Getting back in tune with each other might take intentional rehearsal time— remembering why they fell in love in the first place, practicing what they did to win each other's love, and praising God for the gift of their spouse and the melody he or she brings.

> "Courting gets you married and courting keeps you married."
>
> —A husband of 34 years

1. What do these Bible verses say about married love?

Place me like a seal over your heart, like a seal on your arm; for love is as strong as death, its jealousy unyielding as the grave. It burns like blazing fire, like a mighty flame. Many waters cannot quench love; rivers cannot wash it away. (Song of Solomon 8:6–7 NIV)

2. What promises do couples usually make in their wedding vows?

3. List some specific ways a couple can keep their focus on their relationship and not get distracted by other demands.

4. Proverbs 17:22 (NIV) says, "A cheerful heart is good medicine." How has a sense of humor helped your marriage through the years?

Love Serves

Because of His love, we see Jesus' total commitment to serving His Father, His disciples, and sacrificially serving mankind. That becomes the model for us, including in our marriage.

5. John 13:34-35 says, "A new commandment I give to you, that you love one another: just as I have loved you, you also are to love one another. By this all people will know that you are my disciples, if you have love for one another."

   In what ways are we to imitate Jesus in our marriages?

6. Read Philippians 2:3–4, "Do nothing from rivalry or conceit, but in humility count others more significant than yourselves. Let each of you look not only to his own interests, but also to the interests of others."

How can one spouse serve the other in love?

keystone principle

When you serve each other in marriage,
you are demonstrating the love of Christ.

Love is Sacred

Case Study

Understanding the commitment and love required by elder care giving, Ray and Lydia both wondered how they would be able to care for each other if the need arose. They were encouraged by an article about Dr. Robertson McQuilkin, describing how he sacrificially cared for his wife, Muriel, for years in her struggle with Alzheimer's. Dr. McQuilkin's attitude was, "I love Muriel . . . I don't have to care for her. I get to! It is a high honor to care for so wonderful a person."[2]

Read the case study aloud and answer the questions that follow.

Ray and Lydia took Dr. McQuilkin's example to heart, feeling confident that if they needed to care for each other through some illness, God would give them the grace to endure.

Ray and Lydia's desire is to reflect God's love in a marriage where each spouse is totally committed to the other. That is, not a "contract" marriage but a "covenant." The difference being a contract is an agreement where each person fulfills specified tasks or the agreement is broken; a covenant is forever binding, no matter what, and is clearly displayed by God in the Bible. A marriage that is a contract, a 50/50 marriage, is one that can be broken if one spouse does not live up to the standards of the other. A marriage that is a covenant, a 100/100 marriage, is one in which both spouses love "till death parts us," no matter what.

7. How does the McQuilkins' marriage demonstrate a covenant marriage?

8. What does the Bible say in the following verses about the foundations of marriage?

   Let marriage be held in honor among all, and let the marriage bed be undefiled, for God will judge the sexually immoral and adulterous. (Hebrews 13:4)

   Let each one of you love his wife as himself, and let the wife see that she respects her husband. (Ephesians 5:33)

Just as you seek to grow—to be teachable—in other areas of your spiritual life, you can grow in the understanding of what it takes to have a vibrant godly marriage. There are good marriage enrichment books available, as well as helpful seminars, getaways, video trainings and Christian counseling. Check the "Recommended Resources" for these ideas. Just because you have been married a long time doesn't mean it's too late to enhance your relationship.

keystone principle

Love in marriage is not just an emotion,
it is a sacred commitment to God and your spouse.

Close your group time with this benediction, "May the Lord make your love increase and overflow for each other and for everyone else, just as ours does for you. May he strengthen your hearts so that you will be blameless and holy in the presence of our God and Father when our Lord Jesus comes with all his holy ones" (1 Thessalonians 3:12–13 NIV). In Jesus' name, Amen.

make a date

Set a time for you and your spouse to complete the couple's project together before the next group meeting.

....
date

....
time

....
location

Scan this code for additional content.

Or visit FamilyLife.com/connect.

couple's project

On Your Own

Love Letter[3]

Write the answers to the following questions in the form of a letter:

- What qualities most attracted me to you when we first met?
- What qualities do I most appreciate about you now?
- How have our differences helped me grow spiritually and emotionally?
- What steps will I commit to take to love God and you more?

With Your Spouse

1. Exchange letters. (Decide whether you want to read them aloud or to yourselves.)

2. Discuss your letters. What surprised you? What meant the most to you?

3. Pray together. Take turns thanking God for each other.

Remember to take your calendar to the next session for Make a Date.

Recommended Resources

The Five Love Languages by Dr. Gary Chapman
Love and Respect by Dr. Emerson Eggerichs
Rekindling the Romance by Dennis and Barbara Rainey
Sacred Marriage by Gary Thomas
Movies: *Fireproof* and *Courageous*

~5~
Finish Well

Your marriage will impact generations to come. Will you leave a godly legacy for those who follow you?

warm-up

Choose one of the following to share with your group:

- What is your favorite Bible verse or story?
- What hymn or worship song has become your favorite, and why?

Project Report

Share one thing you learned from last session's couple's project.

master designs

The journey of midlife can be joyous as well as overwhelming. Many times the challenges seem too difficult. It is in those times that we can apply the old lesson of "Stop, Look, and Listen" to our thought life. *Stop*, and be still. Take time to *look* within, around, and up for understanding and help. And, *listen* to what God has to say about who you are and what you should do next.

Stop

Your life can become so busy that you fail to take time to stop and rest—to spend time with the Lord, with your spouse, and with others.

1. "Be still before the LORD and wait patiently for him" (Psalm 37:7). What does it mean to "be still"?

2. Why is it important to take the time to be still during your weekly schedule?

Look

This study has involved "taking a look" in many directions:

- Look Inward—In session one, we examined current challenges.
- Look Upward—In session two, we studied lessons from God.
- Look Backward—In session three, we remembered God's faithfulness.
- Look Outward—In session four, we examined how to love and serve others.
- Look Forward—In session five, we will look at "next steps."

First Samuel 16:7 has something to say about how God looks at us, "For the LORD sees not as man sees: man looks on the outward appearance, but the LORD looks on the heart."

3. Are people remembered for what they look like or for their character? Explain your answer.

Have someone read the following aloud to the group:

> I asked God for strength, that I might achieve;
> I was made weak, that I might learn humbly to obey.
> I asked for health, that I might do greater things;
> I was given infirmity, that I might do better things.
> I asked for riches, that I might be happy;
> I was given poverty, that I might be wise.
> I asked for power, that I might have the praise of men;
> I was given weakness, that I might feel the need of God.
> I asked for all things, that I might enjoy life;
> I was given life, that I might enjoy all things.
> I got nothing that I asked for, but everything I hoped for.
> Almost despite myself, my unspoken prayers were answered.
> I am among all men most richly blessed.

4. What attitudes of contentment and teachability would God see in the character of the person who wrote this (believed to have been a soldier in the Civil War)?

Listen

Perhaps, you are looking forward to years of peace and quiet, or perhaps, you are facing many challenges. In either case, you can listen to what God has to say in His Word about His presence, His provision, and His purpose.

God's Presence—Joy is found in seeing God's hand in your circumstances and in knowing the joy that comes from His presence. Hebrews 13:5 states that God has said, "I will never leave you nor forsake you."

Satan, the enemy of your soul, would love to deceive you into believing that you are alone. The result of believing that lie is isolation—and isolation is the enemy of oneness in marriage.

5. Read Joshua 1:9, "Have I not commanded you? Be strong and courageous. Do not be frightened, and do not be dismayed, for the Lord your God is with you wherever you go."

   What does this verse say about God's presence in your lives? How does His presence strengthen your marriage?

God's Provision—If you are not careful, you can spend your second-half years in worry. The apostle Paul, in his letter to the Philippians, wrote, "Do not be anxious about anything, but in everything by prayer and supplication with thanksgiving let your requests be made known to God. And the peace of God, which surpasses all understanding, will guard your hearts and your minds in Christ Jesus" (Philippians 4:6–7).

6. Paul goes on to say in Philippians 4:19, "And my God will supply every need of yours according to his riches in glory in Christ Jesus." What does this verse say about God's sovereign provision for your lives?

God's Purpose—Our relationship with God is central in building a lasting, satisfying marriage. We acknowledge that the Christian life does not end with salvation. The emphasis is on spiritual growth—becoming like Christ. Each of us must be responsible for our own spiritual growth. At the same time, it is God's plan that in marriage we are to share spiritual growth and ministry. By talking, praying, studying, serving, and dreaming, we can accomplish God's purposes.[1]

How well you accomplish God's purposes in your marriage becomes part of the legacy you leave to future generations. "Future generations" could mean your own physical descendants or others within your sphere of influence. When given the opportunity to teach or mentor younger couples about God's plan for marriage and the family, you are investing in their lives. If you have used your talents, gifts, finances, and prayers to influence others in their Christian faith, you are leaving behind a lasting legacy of holiness.

7. What legacies are found in the following Old Testament psalm and New Testament declaration?

O God, from my youth you have taught me, and I still proclaim your wondrous deeds. So even to old age and gray hairs, O God, do not forsake me, until I proclaim your might to another generation, your power to all those to come. (Psalm 71:17–18)

However, I consider my life worth nothing to me, if only I may finish the race and complete the task the Lord Jesus has given me—the task of testifying to the gospel of God's grace. (Acts 20:24 NIV)

keystone principle
*Only through the grace of God can you
leave a legacy of holiness.*

8. How has your view of life and marriage in the second half changed as a result of this study?

Spend time as a group thanking God and praying for future generations.

Close your group time together with this benediction, "Now may the God of peace who brought again from the dead our Lord Jesus, the great shepherd of the sheep, by the blood of the eternal covenant, equip you with everything good that you may do his will, working in us that which is pleasing in his sight, through Jesus Christ, to whom be glory forever and ever. Amen" (Hebrews 13:20–21).

make a date

Set a time for you and your spouse to complete the last couple's project of the study.

....
date

....
time

....
location

Scan this code for additional content.

Or visit FamilyLife.com/connect.

couple's project

On Your Own

1. What have you learned from this study?

2. Are there issues in your life or marriage that are preventing you from building a legacy of holiness? What are those issues?

3. What steps are you willing to take in order to work on those issues?

4. Pray for God to equip you to accomplish His will in these steps.

5. Ponder these questions from each of the ACTS steps of prayer (see p. 16):

   - Adoration: How has God's goodness carried you through difficult times?
   - Confession: In what ways did the time of confession in "For God's Eyes Only," from session three, give you a sense of freedom?
   - Thanksgiving: What are you thankful for in your marriage that you hope to pass on to future generations?
   - Supplication: How can you pray for future generations?

6. OPTIONAL: Write letters of blessings to your spouse, your children, and those who have significantly helped you in your life. Tell them why you are grateful for their influence and what you most admire about them. This exercise is very important, as these letters, given to special people in your life, can become treasured mementos for them. This exercise can also become a habit of regularly giving encouraging messages to others because of the ways they have helped you.

With Your Spouse

1. Discuss your responses to the questions you answered on your own.

2. How can you help each other live well in the second half and build a legacy of holiness?

3. How can you help other couples do the same?

4. Decide on two action points that, as a couple, you would like to accomplish together in order to leave a godly legacy.

5. Pray together, and ask God to

- forgive you for mistakes and hurts in the past,
- receive your thanksgiving for how you are growing in your relationship with Him and with each other,
- teach you how you can continue to grow closer during the remaining years of your life together,
- reveal how He can use you to minister to other couples in their marriages,
- reveal how He can use you to disciple other couples to be leaders in spiritual movements—around your community or around the world, and
- close by thanking Him for how He is going to continue to work in your marriage to finish well.

To God be the glory!

Recommended Resources

The Art of Marriage® from FamilyLife
Don't Waste Your Life by John Piper
Extreme Grandparenting by Tim Kimmel
Weekend to Remember® marriage getaway from FamilyLife

where do you go from here?

We hope that you have benefited from this study in the Art of Marriage Connect Series and that your marriage will continue to grow as you both submit your lives to Jesus Christ and build according to His designs. We also hope that you will reach out to strengthen other marriages in your local church and community. Your influence is needed.

A favorite World War II story illustrates this point clearly.

The year was 1940. The French army had just collapsed under Hitler's onslaught. The Dutch had folded, overwhelmed by the Nazi regime. The Belgians had surrendered. And the British army was trapped on the coast of France in the channel port of Dunkirk.

Two hundred and twenty thousand of Britain's finest young men seemed doomed to die, turning the English Channel red with their blood. The Fuehrer's troops, only miles away in the hills of France, didn't realize how close to victory they actually were.

Any attempt at rescue seemed futile in the time remaining. A thin British navy—the professionals—told King George VI that they could save 17,000 troops at best. The House of Commons was warned to prepare for "hard and heavy tidings."

Politicians were paralyzed. The king was powerless. And the Allies could only watch as spectators from a distance. Then, as the doom of the British army seemed imminent, a strange fleet appeared on the horizon of the English Channel—the wildest assortment of boats perhaps ever assembled in history: trawlers, tugs, scows, fishing sloops, lifeboats, pleasure craft, smacks and coasters, sailboats, even the London fire-brigade flotilla, ships manned by civilian volunteers—English fathers joining in the rescue of Britain's exhausted, bleeding sons.

William Manchester writes in his epic novel, *The Last Lion*, that what happened in 1940 at Dunkirk seems like a miracle. Not only were most of the British soldiers rescued, but 118,000 other Allied troops as well.

Today, the Christian home is much like those troops at Dunkirk—pressured, trapped, demoralized, and in need of help. The Christian community may be much like England—waiting for professionals to step in and save the family. But the problem is much too large for them to solve alone.

We need an all-out effort by men and women "sailing" to rescue the exhausted and wounded families. We need an outreach effort by common couples with faith in an uncommon God. For too long, married couples within the church have abdicated to those in full-time vocational ministry the privilege and responsibility of influencing others.

We challenge you to invest your lives in others, to join in the rescue. You and other couples around the world can team together to build thousands of marriages and families and, in doing so, continue to strengthen your own.

Be a HomeBuilder

Looking for more ways to help people build their marriages and families? Here are some practical ways you can make a difference in families today:

- Gather a group of couples and lead them through this study. Consider challenging others to form additional groups by doing another small-group study in the Art of Marriage Connect Series.
- Host the Art of Marriage video event or the Art of Marriage small-group series in your church or community.
- Consider using the *JESUS* film as an outreach. For more information contact FamilyLife.

- Host a dinner party. Invite families from your neighborhood to your home, and as a couple, share your faith in Christ.
- If you have attended FamilyLife's Weekend to Remember marriage getaway, consider offering to assist your pastor in counseling engaged couples, using the material you received.

For more information about these ministry opportunities, contact your local church or

FamilyLife
PO Box 7111
Little Rock, AR 72223
1-800-FL-TODAY
FamilyLife.com

our problems, God's answers

Every couple has to deal with problems in marriage—communication problems, money problems, difficulties with sexual intimacy, and more. Learning how to handle these issues is important to cultivating a strong and loving relationship.

The Big Problem

One basic problem is at the heart of every other problem in marriage, and it's too big for any person to deal with on his or her own. The problem is separation from God. If you want to experience life and marriage the way they were designed to be, you need a vital relationship with the God who created you.

But sin separates us from God. Some try to deal with sin by working hard to become better people. They may read books on how to control anger, or they may resolve to stop cheating or lying, but in their hearts they know—we all know—that the sin problem runs much deeper than bad habits and will take more than our best behavior to overcome it. In reality, we have rebelled against God. We have ignored Him and have decided to run our lives in a way that makes sense to us, thinking that our ideas and plans are better than His.

For all have sinned and fall short of the glory of God. (Romans 3:23)

What does it mean to "fall short of the glory of God"? It means that none of us have trusted and treasured God the way we should. We have sought to satisfy ourselves with other things and have treated them as more valuable than God. We have gone our own way. According to the Bible, we have to pay a penalty for our sin. We cannot simply do things the way we choose and hope it will be okay with God. Following our own plans leads to our destruction.

> There is a way that seems right to a man, but its end is the way to death. (Proverbs 14:12)

> For the wages of sin is death. (Romans 6:23)

The penalty for sin is that we are separated from God's love. God is holy, and we are sinful. No matter how hard we try, we cannot come up with some plan, like living a good life or even trying to do what the Bible says, and hope that we can avoid the penalty.

God's Solution to Sin

Thankfully, God has a way to solve our dilemma. He became a man through the person of Jesus Christ. Jesus lived a holy life in perfect obedience to God's plan. He also willingly died on a cross to pay our penalty for sin. Then He proved that He is more powerful than sin or death by rising from the dead. He alone has the power to overrule the penalty for our sin.

> Jesus said to him, "I am the way, and the truth, and the life. No one comes to the Father except through me." (John 14:6)

> But God shows his love for us in that while we were still sinners, Christ died for us. (Romans 5:8)

> For the wages of sin is death, but the free gift of God is eternal life in Christ Jesus our Lord. (Romans 6:23)

The death and resurrection of Jesus have fixed our sin problem. He has bridged the gap between God and us. He is calling us to come to Him and to give up our flawed plans for running our lives. He wants us to trust God and His plan.

Accepting God's Solution

If you recognize that you are separated from God, He is calling you to confess your sins. All of us have made messes of our lives, because we have stubbornly preferred our ideas and plans to His. As a result, we deserve to be cut off from God's love and His care for us. But God has promised that if we will acknowledge that we have rebelled against His plan, He will forgive us and fix our sin problem.

> But to all who did receive him, who believed in his name, he gave the right to become children of God. (John 1:12)

> For by grace you have been saved through faith. And this is not your own doing; it is the gift of God, not a result of works, so that no one may boast. (Ephesians 2:8–9)

When the Bible talks about receiving Christ, it means we acknowledge that we are sinners and that we can't fix the problem ourselves. It means we turn away from our sin. And it means we trust Christ to forgive our sins and to make us the kind of people He wants us to be. It's not enough to intellectually believe that Christ is the Son of God. We must trust in Him and His plan for our lives by faith, as an act of the will.

Are things right between you and God, with Him and His plan at the center of your life? Or is life spinning out of control as you seek to make your own way?

If you have been trying to make your own way, you can decide to change today. You can turn to Christ and allow Him to transform your life. All you need to do is talk to Him and tell Him what is stirring in your mind and in your heart. If you've never done this, consider taking the steps listed here:

- Do you agree that you need God? Tell Him.
- Have you made a mess of your life by following your own plan? Tell God.
- Do you want God to forgive you? Ask Him.
- Do you believe that Jesus' death on the cross and His resurrection from the dead gave Him the power to fix your sin problem and to grant you the free gift of eternal life? Tell God.

- Are you ready to acknowledge that God's plan for your life is better than any plan you could come up with? Tell Him.
- Do you agree that God has the right to be the Lord and Master of your life? Tell Him.

"Seek the LORD while he may be found; call upon him while he is near." (Isaiah 55:6)

Here is a suggested prayer:

Lord Jesus, I need You. Thank You for dying on the cross for my sins. I receive You as my Savior and Lord. Thank You for forgiving my sins and giving me eternal life. Make me the kind of person You want me to be.

The Christian Life

For the person who is a follower of Christ—a Christian—the penalty for sin is paid in full. But the effects of sin continue throughout our lives.

If we say we have no sin, we deceive ourselves, and the truth is not in us. (1 John 1:8)

For I do not do the good I want, but the evil I do not want is what I keep on doing. (Romans 7:19)

The effects of sin carry over into our marriages, as well. Even Christians struggle to maintain solid, God-honoring marriages. Most couples eventually realize they can't do it on their own. But with God's help, they can succeed.

leader's notes

about leading an art of marriage connect group

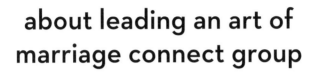

What is the leader's job?

Your role is more of a facilitator than a teacher. A teacher usually does most of the talking and instructing, whereas a facilitator encourages people to think and to discover what the Bible says. You should help group members feel comfortable, and keep the discussion moving forward.

Is there a structure to the sessions?

Yes, each session is composed of three sections. **Warm-Up** (5–10 minutes): The purpose of the Warm-Up is to help people unwind from a busy day and get to know one another better. Typically, the Warm-Up starts with an exercise that is fun but also introduces the topic of the session. **Master Designs** (45–50 minutes): This is the heart of the study when people answer questions related to the topic and look to God's Word for understanding. Some of the questions are to be discussed between spouses and others with the whole group. **Couple's Project** (60 minutes): This project is the unique application that couples will work on between the group meetings. Each project contains two sections: (1) On Your Own—questions for husbands and wives to answer individually and (2) With Your Spouse—an opportunity for couples to share their answers with each other and to make application in their lives and marriages.

What is the best setting and time schedule for this study?

This study is designed as a small-group, home Bible study. However, it can be adapted for more structured settings like a Sunday school class. Here are some suggestions for using this study in various settings:

In a small group

To create a friendly and comfortable atmosphere, we recommend you do this study in a home setting. In many cases, the couple that leads the study also serves as host, but sometimes involving another couple as host is a good idea. Choose the option you believe will work best for your group, taking into account factors such as the number of couples participating and the location.

Each session is designed as a sixty-minute study, but we recommend a ninety-minute block of time to allow for more relaxed conversation and refreshments. Be sure to keep in mind one of the cardinal rules of a small group: good groups start and end on time. Everyone's time is valuable, and your group will appreciate you respecting this.

In a Sunday school class

If you want to use the study in a class setting, you need to adapt it in two important ways: (1) You should focus on the content of the Master Designs section of each session. That is the heart of the session. (2) Many Sunday school classes use a teacher format instead of a small-group format. If this study is used in a class setting, the class should adapt to a small-group dynamic. This will involve an interactive, discussion-based format and may also require a class to break into multiple smaller groups.

What is the best size group?

We recommend from four to seven couples (including you and your spouse). If more people are interested than you can accommodate, consider asking someone to lead a second group. If you have a large group, you may find it beneficial to break into smaller subgroups on occasion. This helps you cover the material in a timely fashion and allows for optimum interaction and participation within the group.

What about refreshments?

Many groups choose to serve refreshments, which helps create an environment of fellowship. If you plan to include refreshments, here are a couple of suggestions: (1) For the first session or two you should provide the refreshments. Then involve the group by having people sign up to bring them on later dates. (2) Consider starting your group with a short time of informal fellowship and refreshments (15–20 minutes). Then move into the study. If couples are late, they may miss the food but should not disrupt the study. (3) You may also want to have refreshments available again at the end of your meeting to encourage fellowship. But remember to respect the group members' time by ending the session on schedule and allowing anyone who needs to leave to do so gracefully.

What about child care?

Groups handle this differently, depending on their needs. Here are a couple of options you may want to consider:

- Have people be responsible for making their own arrangements.
- As a group, hire someone to provide child care and have all the children watched in one location.

What about prayer?

Prayer is an important part of a small group. However, as the leader, you need to be sensitive to people's comfort levels with praying in front of others. Never call on people to pray aloud unless you know they are comfortable doing this. You can take creative approaches, such as modeling prayer, calling for volunteers, and letting people state their prayers in the form of finishing a sentence. A prayer list can also be a helpful tool. You should lead the prayer time, but allow other couples to create, update, and distribute prayer lists as their ministry to the group.

about the leader's notes

The sessions in this study can be easily led without a lot of preparation time; however, Leader's Notes are provided to assist you when needed. The categories within the Leader's Notes are as follows:

objectives

The objectives focus on the issues that will be presented in each session.

notes and tips

This section provides general ideas, helps, and suggestions about the session. You may want to create a checklist of things to include in each session.

master designs commentary

This section contains notes that relate to the Master Designs questions, but not every question will have a commentary note. The number of the commentary note corresponds to the number of the question it relates to. (For example, the Leader's Notes, session 1, number 6 in the Master Designs Commentary section relates back to study session 1, Master Designs, question 6.)

session one
Threats to Oneness

objectives

Marriage in the second half of life brings unique challenges. Through this season a couple has the opportunity to examine their lives and determine the appropriate next steps to leave a godly legacy. This first session introduces the couples to threats to oneness in their marriages.

In this session, couples will

- meet their group,
- identify the threats to marriage in midlife,
- share personal insights regarding this season of marriage,
- evaluate the threats that have touched their lives, and
- learn steps to grow in oneness.

notes and tips

1. As part of the first session, you may want to review the ground rules (see page vi in the Welcome section).

2. The group leader may choose to collect the names, phone numbers, and e-mail addresses of the group members for distribution within the group.

3. Because this is the first session, make a special point to tell the group about the importance of the Couple's Project. Encourage each couple to "make a date" for a time before the next meeting to complete the project. Mention that you will ask about this during the Warm-Up at the next session.

4. If there is room, you may want to remind the group that because this study is just underway, they can still invite another couple to join.

5. You may want to offer a closing prayer instead of asking others to pray aloud. Many people are uncomfortable praying in front of others, and unless you already know your group well, it may be wise to venture slowly into various methods of prayer.

6. The couple identified as Ray and Lydia in several case studies is a fictional composite. They represent the multiple issues that many couples encounter during the second-half season of marriage.

master designs commentary

Here is some additional information about various Master Designs questions. (Note: The numbers below correspond to the Master Designs question they relate to. Notes are not included for every question.) If you share any of these points, be sure to do so in a manner that does not stifle discussion by making yourself the authority with the only right answers. Begin your comments by saying things like, "One thing I notice in this passage is . . ." or, "I think another reason for this might be . . ."

1. Since the group is just starting and may not know each other well, be prepared to share a lesson learned from your years together. For example, if you struggled with infertility early on in your marriage, you might share how you learned patience and how to comfort each other, and now have the ability to comfort others in that same situation. In 2 Corinthians 1:3–4, Paul tells us, "Blessed be the God and Father of our Lord Jesus Christ, the Father of mercies and God of all comfort, who comforts us in all our affliction, so that we may be able to comfort those who are in any affliction, with the comfort with which we ourselves are comforted by God."

Another example might be if your career required you to relocate several times (for example, the military), you might share how you learned to adapt and make new friends. Even though the demands were many, you learned to appreciate many parts of the world and the struggles of others. Now you are able to help younger couples who face similar challenges.

2. Within any group of midlife marriages there will be a wide variety of circumstances that couples are dealing with—health concerns, finances, adult children, grandparenting, etc. Make sure that the couples have time to share various transitions but do not linger on any one concern.

3. This question is meant to be a general one. If couples start sharing personal expectations and disappointments make sure you guard the conversation from any one couple dominating the discussion time.

8. Oneness in a Christian marriage means a spiritual union between a husband and wife—which is the best relationship to have. With a spiritual union, you can both work in the power of the Holy Spirit to demonstrate tenderness, compassion, like-mindedness, love, purpose, unselfishness, and humility.

Closing in benediction—Since the group is new, the group leader may want to read the benediction for the group. In weeks to come, this responsibility of closing the group in prayer can be shared.

session two
Live Well

objectives

With an understanding of the threats to their midlife marriage, couples can now examine the current state of their spiritual wellness.

In this session couples will

- explore three important aspects of learning and how they affect a midlife marriage,
- discuss the value of growing in knowledge of the Lord, and
- go over a list of relevant topics for agreement in how they are being handled in their marriage.

notes and tips

1. This session introduces practical realities of life lessons passed down from the Bible and previous generations. Couples may be surprised that Scripture offers so much help in dealing with modern issues such as wealth, morality, busyness, and worry. They may also be amazed at how many of them struggle with discontentment and spiritual laziness. This session will encourage couples to see value in learning more about God.

2. If someone in this session has joined the group for the first time, give a brief summary of the main points of session one. Also, be sure to introduce those who do not know each other. Consider giving new couples the chance to tell when and where they met.

3. If your group has decided to use a prayer list, make sure this is covered.

4. If refreshments are planned for this session, make sure arrangements for them have been made.

5. If you told the group during the first session that you would be asking them to share something they learned from the first Couple's Project, be sure to ask them. This is an important way for you to establish an environment of accountability.

6. Group members will need their Bibles for this session. You might want to have some extra Bibles available for those who do not bring one.

7. Remember the importance of starting and ending on time.

master designs commentary

3. We all struggle with discontentment (and disillusionment or disappointment) at one time or another. Our culture makes it worse with advertising—which is designed to cultivate discontentment. You can relate this question to session one when you discussed "Divisive Attitudes" as a threat to oneness.

8. Some couples have never prayed together. Taking a moment to go over the ACTS acronym may be helpful as a model for prayer (see p. 16).

9. Church involvement is vital to a couple's spiritual health and growth. Getting plugged into a local church will benefit them in many ways for the rest of their life. Encourage couples to seek out fellowship and worship in churches that you are prepared to recommend.

session three
Remember Well

objectives

Often in the busyness of our days, we do not pause to reflect on God's goodness in our lives. Couples need to look back over their years together, however many or few they may be, and examine the importance of faith.

In this session couples will

- read Bible verses calling them to remember God's faithfulness,
- discuss the importance of forgiveness—received and given, and
- be given the opportunity to receive Jesus Christ as Lord and Savior.

notes and tips

1. Since this is the third session, your group members have probably warmed up to one another. But they may not yet feel free to be completely open and honest about their past, unless they already know each other well. Don't force the issue. Continue to encourage couples to attend and to complete their projects.

2. This session can be the most transformational of the entire study, because it addresses the importance of establishing a relationship with God through Jesus Christ. Please persevere through any awkwardness you may sense, and boldly present this life-changing decision to your group.

3. You may want to ask for a volunteer to close the session in prayer, including the benediction. Check ahead of time with people you think might be comfortable praying aloud.

4. Congratulations! With the completion of this session, you are more than halfway through this study. It's time for a checkup: How are you feeling? How is the group doing? What has worked well so far? What things would you consider changing as you head into the remaining sessions?

master designs commentary

1. It is important to know that God calls us to acts of remembrance—in both the Old Testament and New Testament. You might want to mention some Bible stories in which there is a time of remembrance, such as Passover.

7. The story of John Newton is an example of a changed life because of repentance and faith in Jesus Christ. Introducing Ray to the story of "Amazing Grace" serves as a means for talking with your group about the gospel. You can also encourage your group members to read "Our Problems, God's Answers" beginning on page 57.

session four
Love Well

objectives

What does love look like in the second half of life? Some group members may have experienced divorce but want to "get it right" this time. This session can be one of real affirmation and encouragement for all the couples.

In this session couples will

- look back and share what brought them together in the first place,
- understand the connection between how Jesus loved others by serving them and how we can love our spouse and others by serving them,
- learn the difference between a covenant and a contract and how that applies to marriage, and
- bless their spouse with a love letter.

notes and tips

1. Make sure to pray for each couple in your group throughout this week.

2. You and your spouse may want to mail notes of encouragement to the couples in your group, thanking them for their commitment and contribution to the group.

3. Make sure you start and end your group on time. This shows respect for everyone's schedules.

master designs commentary

3. Be careful not to spend too much time discussing the distractions. You want the group members to help one another by sharing suggestions for keeping the focus on the relationship.

5. The Greek language, in which most of the New Testament was written, has four words for *love*: phileo (friendship), agape (unconditional love), eros (romance), and storge (affection). To better grasp the concept of love, we need to describe the different aspects of it through romance, service, and sacredness.

session five
Finish Well

objectives

The second half of life offers a wonderful opportunity to be intentional about the priority of relationships. The couples in your study have spheres of influence. What will their legacy be within those relationships?

In this session couples will

- discuss the importance of taking time to spend with the Lord, their spouse, and others;
- discuss God's presence, provision, and purpose;
- share how the study has affected them personally and as a couple; and
- develop next steps in shaping a God-honoring legacy.

notes and tips

1. In this final session, encourage couples to take steps beyond this study to keep their marriages growing. Perhaps, they could begin with having a date night each week, attending a marriage conference, reading a book on marriage together, or going on a retreat to focus on prayer for their family.

2. Our hope for this session is that the couples will end the study on high ground—looking back at their lives with new understanding and looking forward with new hope. Sadly, after many years of marriage, some couples become discouraged and give up on anything beyond the status quo. The subject matter of this lesson will challenge them to see the importance of finding purpose and

joy in the second half years they have together. We hope they have learned thus far that life is not about ourselves—it's all about God and living for Him. They can demonstrate and declare His faithfulness to future generations. That is a godly legacy.

3. Your group may want to plan one more meeting—a party to celebrate the completion of this study.

4. You might ask one person or couple to share what this study or group has meant to them.

master designs commentary

4. Here is another option for use as a Case Study. Written on the eve of cancer surgery, theologian John Piper's article, "Don't Waste Your Cancer," challenges us to look for ways to mature through suffering. Your group could read and discuss this list—and can replace the word "cancer" with whatever struggle they are currently facing:

    - You will waste your cancer if you do not believe it is designed for you by God.
    - You will waste your cancer if you believe it is a curse and not a gift.
    - You will waste your cancer if you seek comfort from your odds rather than from God.
    - You will waste your cancer if you refuse to think about death.
    - You will waste your cancer if you think that "beating" cancer means staying alive, rather than cherishing Christ.
    - You will waste your cancer if you spend too much time reading about cancer and not enough time reading about God.
    - You will waste your cancer if you let it drive you into solitude, instead of deepen your relationships with manifest affection.
    - You will waste your cancer if you grieve as those who have no hope.

- You will waste your cancer if you treat sin as casually as before.
- You will waste your cancer if you fail to use it as a means of witness to the truth and glory of Christ.

7. Make sure the couples understand that a legacy will be marked by commitment to the Lord and each other, persistence through life's challenges, and declaring the gospel of Jesus Christ to future generations.

notes

Session 2

1. Linda Dillow, *Calm My Anxious Heart: A Woman's Guide to Finding Contentment* (Colorado Springs: NavPress, 1998), 101.

2. Steve Farrar, *Finishing Strong: Going the Distance for Your Family* (Sisters, OR: Multnomah Publishers, Inc., 1995), 133.

3. Gary and Betsy Ricucci, *Love That Lasts: When Marriage Meets Grace* (Wheaton, IL: Crossway Books, 2006), 26.

Session 3

1. Dennis Rainey, "For God's Eyes Only," *Building Your Marriage to Last* (Little Rock, AR: FamilyLife Publishing, 2010), 65.

2. Dietrich Bonhoeffer, *Letters and Papers from Prison* (New York: Touchstone, 1997), 46–47.

Session 4

1. Jim and Barbara Grunseth, *Remember the Rowboats: Anchor your Marriage to Christ* (Minneapolis: River City Press, Inc., 2008), 66–67.

2. Robertson McQuilkin, *A Promise Kept: The Story of an Unforgettable Love* (Carol Stream, IL: Tyndale, 1998), 23.

3. Dennis Rainey, *Building Your Marriage to Last* (Little Rock, AR: FamilyLife Publishing, 1987, 2010), 25–27.

Session 5

1. Gary Chapman, *Covenant Marriage: Building Communication and Intimacy* (Nashville: B&H Publishing Group, 2003), 210.

more tools for leaders

Thank you for your efforts to help people develop their marriages and families using biblical principles. We recognize the influence that one person—or couple—can have on another, and we'd like to help you multiply your ministry.

FamilyLife is pleased to offer a wide range of resources in various formats. Visit us online at FamilyLife.com, where you will find information about our

- getaways and events, featuring Weekend to Remember®, offered in cities throughout the United States;
- multimedia resources for small groups, churches, and community networking such as The Art of Marriage®, Stepping Up®, and FamilyLife Blended®;
- interactive products for parents, couples, small-group leaders, and one-to-one mentors; and
- blogs, forums, and other online connections.

God can turn **any marriage** into a **masterpiece.**

Making marriage work is a divinely inspired art form. The Art of Marriage® video event incorporates expert teaching, engaging stories, real-life testimonies, humorous vignettes, and projects for couples in an expanded video-based format. Crafted with church or community settings in mind, this one-and-a-half-day event casts a compelling vision for marriage as God designed.

FAMILYLIFE® presents

the art of ♥ **marriage**®

a six-session video event

To learn more, visit
TheArtofMarriage.com

also available in **Spanish**

The Art of Marriage® small-group series

Over 700,000 have experienced stronger marriages as a result of The Art of Marriage video event. Now the same great content is available in a format perfect for Sunday school groups, home Bible study groups, or any other small-group setting. In six sessions, we weave together expert teaching, real-life stories, and man-on-the-street interviews to portray the hope and beauty of God's design for marriage.

The Art of Marriage small-group series kit includes:

- One DVD featuring six 20–25 minute video sessions

- A leader's guide

- Two workbooks that include small-group discussion questions, date night suggestions for couples, articles, and more.

FAMILYLIFE® presents

the art of ♥ marriage®

About FamilyLife®

At FamilyLife we understand how good marriages and home life can be. And how challenging. That's why we work to provide tools and events that will help you build on a solid foundation, repair what has been broken, or reclaim what has been lost—all from a biblical perspective. Our books and resources offer practical, proven solutions to support you after that late-night argument with the kids, in the midst of a crushing confession, or when you simply need a new date-night idea. You'll find help for every stage of the journey, from pre-wedding jitters to the empty-nest years and beyond.

Through each ministry offering, including Weekend to Remember®, Stepping Up®, The Art of Marriage®, FamilyLife Blended®, and *FamilyLife Today*® radio broadcasts, FamilyLife shares biblical designs to help families stay together—and value their togetherness—no matter what the future holds.

FamilyLife is a donor-supported ministry. We rely on friends like you, who recognize the critical role of the family, to help us reach even more marriages and homes.

Would you consider joining us in our mission? Please visit **FamilyLife.com/GetInvolved** to see the many ways you can partner with FamilyLife to help families across America and throughout the world. Thank you.

 facebook.com/familylifeministry   @FamilyLifeToday